DEDICATION

This Date Night Planner is dedicated to all the lovers out there who love to plan some time away, and document their findings in the process.

You are my inspiration for producing books and I'm honored to be a part of keeping all of your date night notes and records organized.

How to use this Date Night Planner:

This useful date night planner is a must-have for couples that need a break! You will love this easy to use journal to track and record all your going on a date activities.

Each interior page includes space to record & track the following:

1. Going On a Date With - Write down the name or names of all your dates.
2. Month - Use the calendar to write in the month, date night, what, where and when.
3. Things To Do - Stay on task using the space to make a list of pickup, calls to make, sitter to hire.

If you are new to the world of dating or have been at it for a while, this date planning notebook is a must have! Can make a great useful gift for anyone that loves to plan for date night!

Have Fun!

DATE NIGHT PLANNER

Going on a date with;

 1

 2

3

4

 5

6

 7

 8

 9

10

 11

 12

 13

 14

MONTH _____

• • • • • • • • ● ● ● ♡ ● ● ● ● ● • • •

DATE NIGHT	DATE NIGHT	DATE NIGHT
What_____	What_____	What_____
Where_____	Where_____	Where_____
When_____	When_____	When_____

DATE NIGHT	DATE NIGHT	DATE NIGHT
What_____	What_____	What_____
Where_____	Where_____	Where_____
When_____	When_____	When_____

DATE NIGHT	DATE NIGHT	DATE NIGHT
What_____	What_____	What_____
Where_____	Where_____	Where_____
When_____	When_____	When_____

• • • • • • • ● ● ● ♡ ● ● ● ● ● • • •

THINGS TO DO	THINGS TO DO	THINGS TO DO
Pickup	Pickup	Pickup
Calls	Calls	Calls
Sitter	Sitter	Sitter

MONTH _____

• • • • • • • • • ● ● ● ♡ ● ● ● ● • • • •

DATE NIGHT	DATE NIGHT	DATE NIGHT
What _____	What _____	What _____
Where _____	Where _____	Where _____
When _____	When _____	When _____

DATE NIGHT	DATE NIGHT	DATE NIGHT
What _____	What _____	What _____
Where _____	Where _____	Where _____
When _____	When _____	When _____

DATE NIGHT	DATE NIGHT	DATE NIGHT
What _____	What _____	What _____
Where _____	Where _____	Where _____
When _____	When _____	When _____

• • • • • • • • ● ● ● ♡ ● ● ● ● • • • •

THINGS TO DO	THINGS TO DO	THINGS TO DO
Pickup	Pickup	Pickup
Calls	Calls	Calls
Sitter	Sitter	Sitter

MONTH _____

•••••••●●●●●●♡●●●●●••••••

DATE NIGHT

*What*_____

*Where*_____

*When*_____

DATE NIGHT

*What*_____

*Where*_____

*When*_____

DATE NIGHT

*What*_____

*Where*_____

*When*_____

DATE NIGHT

*What*_____

*Where*_____

*When*_____

DATE NIGHT

*What*_____

*Where*_____

*When*_____

DATE NIGHT

*What*_____

*Where*_____

*When*_____

DATE NIGHT

*What*_____

*Where*_____

*When*_____

DATE NIGHT

*What*_____

*Where*_____

*When*_____

DATE NIGHT

*What*_____

*Where*_____

*When*_____

•••••••●●●●●●♡●●●●●••••••

THINGS TO DO

Pickup

Calls

Sitter

THINGS TO DO

Pickup

Calls

Sitter

THINGS TO DO

Pickup

Calls

Sitter

MONTH _____

•••●●●●●●●●♡●●●●●●••••

DATE NIGHT

What_____

Where_____

When_____

DATE NIGHT

What_____

Where_____

When_____

DATE NIGHT

What_____

Where_____

When_____

DATE NIGHT

What_____

Where_____

When_____

DATE NIGHT

What_____

Where_____

When_____

DATE NIGHT

What_____

Where_____

When_____

DATE NIGHT

What_____

Where_____

When_____

DATE NIGHT

What_____

Where_____

When_____

DATE NIGHT

What_____

Where_____

When_____

•••●●●●●●●♡●●●●●●••••

THINGS TO DO

Pickup

Calls

Sitter

THINGS TO DO

Pickup

Calls

Sitter

THINGS TO DO

Pickup

Calls

Sitter

MONTH _____

• • • • • • • ● ● ● ♡ ● ● ● • • • • •

DATE NIGHT

What _____
Where _____
When _____

DATE NIGHT

What _____
Where _____
When _____

DATE NIGHT

What _____
Where _____
When _____

DATE NIGHT

What _____
Where _____
When _____

DATE NIGHT

What _____
Where _____
When _____

DATE NIGHT

What _____
Where _____
When _____

DATE NIGHT

What _____
Where _____
When _____

DATE NIGHT

What _____
Where _____
When _____

DATE NIGHT

What _____
Where _____
When _____

• • • • • • • ● ● ● ♡ ● ● ● • • • • •

THINGS TO DO

Pickup

Calls

Sitter

THINGS TO DO

Pickup

Calls

Sitter

THINGS TO DO

Pickup

Calls

Sitter

MONTH _____

••••••●●●●●♡●●●●●••••

DATE NIGHT

What_____

Where_____

When_____

DATE NIGHT

What_____

Where_____

When_____

DATE NIGHT

What_____

Where_____

When_____

DATE NIGHT

What_____

Where_____

When_____

DATE NIGHT

What_____

Where_____

When_____

DATE NIGHT

What_____

Where_____

When_____

DATE NIGHT

What_____

Where_____

When_____

DATE NIGHT

What_____

Where_____

When_____

DATE NIGHT

What_____

Where_____

When_____

••••••●●●●●♡●●●●●••••

THINGS TO DO

Pickup

Calls

Sitter

THINGS TO DO

Pickup

Calls

Sitter

THINGS TO DO

Pickup

Calls

Sitter

MONTH _____

• • • • • • • • ● ● ● ♡ ● ● ● ● • • • • •

DATE NIGHT

What _____

Where _____

When _____

DATE NIGHT

What _____

Where _____

When _____

DATE NIGHT

What _____

Where _____

When _____

DATE NIGHT

What _____

Where _____

When _____

DATE NIGHT

What _____

Where _____

When _____

DATE NIGHT

What _____

Where _____

When _____

DATE NIGHT

What _____

Where _____

When _____

DATE NIGHT

What _____

Where _____

When _____

DATE NIGHT

What _____

Where _____

When _____

• • • • • • • • ● ● ● ♡ ● ● ● ● • • • • •

THINGS TO DO

Pickup

Calls

Sitter

THINGS TO DO

Pickup

Calls

Sitter

THINGS TO DO

Pickup

Calls

Sitter

MONTH _____

•••••••••●●●●♡●●●●●●••••

DATE NIGHT

What_____

Where_____

When_____

DATE NIGHT

What_____

Where_____

When_____

DATE NIGHT

What_____

Where_____

When_____

DATE NIGHT

What_____

Where_____

When_____

DATE NIGHT

What_____

Where_____

When_____

DATE NIGHT

What_____

Where_____

When_____

DATE NIGHT

What_____

Where_____

When_____

DATE NIGHT

What_____

Where_____

When_____

DATE NIGHT

What_____

Where_____

When_____

•••••••●●●●♡●●●●••••

THINGS TO DO

Pickup

Calls

Sitter

THINGS TO DO

Pickup

Calls

Sitter

THINGS TO DO

Pickup

Calls

Sitter

MONTH _____

•••••●●●●●●♡●●●●•••••

DATE NIGHT

What _____

Where _____

When _____

DATE NIGHT

What _____

Where _____

When _____

DATE NIGHT

What _____

Where _____

When _____

DATE NIGHT

What _____

Where _____

When _____

DATE NIGHT

What _____

Where _____

When _____

DATE NIGHT

What _____

Where _____

When _____

DATE NIGHT

What _____

Where _____

When _____

DATE NIGHT

What _____

Where _____

When _____

DATE NIGHT

What _____

Where _____

When _____

•••••●●●●●♡●●●●●•••••

THINGS TO DO

Pickup

Calls

Sitter

THINGS TO DO

Pickup

Calls

Sitter

THINGS TO DO

Pickup

Calls

Sitter

MONTH _____

•••••••••●●●●♡●●●●●•••••

DATE NIGHT	DATE NIGHT	DATE NIGHT
What _____	What _____	What _____
Where _____	Where _____	Where _____
When _____	When _____	When _____

DATE NIGHT	DATE NIGHT	DATE NIGHT
What _____	What _____	What _____
Where _____	Where _____	Where _____
When _____	When _____	When _____

DATE NIGHT	DATE NIGHT	DATE NIGHT
What _____	What _____	What _____
Where _____	Where _____	Where _____
When _____	When _____	When _____

•••••••••●●●●♡●●●●●•••••

THINGS TO DO	THINGS TO DO	THINGS TO DO
Pickup	Pickup	Pickup
Calls	Calls	Calls
Sitter	Sitter	Sitter

MONTH _____

•••••••●●●●♡●●●●•••••

DATE NIGHT	DATE NIGHT	DATE NIGHT
What _____	*What* _____	*What* _____
Where _____	*Where* _____	*Where* _____
When _____	*When* _____	*When* _____

DATE NIGHT	DATE NIGHT	DATE NIGHT
What _____	*What* _____	*What* _____
Where _____	*Where* _____	*Where* _____
When _____	*When* _____	*When* _____

DATE NIGHT	DATE NIGHT	DATE NIGHT
What _____	*What* _____	*What* _____
Where _____	*Where* _____	*Where* _____
When _____	*When* _____	*When* _____

•••••••●●●●♡●●●●•••••

THINGS TO DO   THINGS TO DO   THINGS TO DO

Pickup   *Pickup*   *Pickup*

Calls   *Calls*   *Calls*

Sitter   *Sitter*   *Sitter*

MONTH _____

•••••••●●●●●●♡●●●●●••••••

DATE NIGHT	DATE NIGHT	DATE NIGHT
What _____	What _____	What _____
Where _____	Where _____	Where _____
When _____	When _____	When _____

DATE NIGHT	DATE NIGHT	DATE NIGHT
What _____	What _____	What _____
Where _____	Where _____	Where _____
When _____	When _____	When _____

DATE NIGHT	DATE NIGHT	DATE NIGHT
What _____	What _____	What _____
Where _____	Where _____	Where _____
When _____	When _____	When _____

•••••●●●●●●♡●●●●●•••••

THINGS TO DO	THINGS TO DO	THINGS TO DO
Pickup	Pickup	Pickup
Calls	Calls	Calls
Sitter	Sitter	Sitter

MONTH _____

•••••••●●●●●♡●●●●•••••

DATE NIGHT

What _____

Where _____

When _____

DATE NIGHT

What _____

Where _____

When _____

DATE NIGHT

What _____

Where _____

When _____

DATE NIGHT

What _____

Where _____

When _____

DATE NIGHT

What _____

Where _____

When _____

DATE NIGHT

What _____

Where _____

When _____

DATE NIGHT

What _____

Where _____

When _____

DATE NIGHT

What _____

Where _____

When _____

DATE NIGHT

What _____

Where _____

When _____

•••••••●●●●●♡●●●●•••••

THINGS TO DO

Pickup

Calls

Sitter

THINGS TO DO

Pickup

Calls

Sitter

THINGS TO DO

Pickup

Calls

Sitter

MONTH _____

•••••••●●●●♡●●●●•••••

DATE NIGHT	DATE NIGHT	DATE NIGHT

What _____ *What* _____ *What* _____

Where _____ *Where* _____ *Where* _____

When _____ *When* _____ *When* _____

DATE NIGHT   DATE NIGHT   DATE NIGHT

What _____ *What* _____ *What* _____

Where _____ *Where* _____ *Where* _____

When _____ *When* _____ *When* _____

DATE NIGHT   DATE NIGHT   DATE NIGHT

What _____ *What* _____ *What* _____

Where _____ *Where* _____ *Where* _____

When _____ *When* _____ *When* _____

•••••••●●●●♡●●●●•••••

THINGS TO DO   THINGS TO DO   THINGS TO DO

Pickup   *Pickup*   *Pickup*

Calls   *Calls*   *Calls*

Sitter   *Sitter*   *Sitter*

MONTH _____

•••••••●●●●●♡●●●●●•••••

DATE NIGHT

What _____

Where _____

When _____

DATE NIGHT

What _____

Where _____

When _____

DATE NIGHT

What _____

Where _____

When _____

DATE NIGHT

What _____

Where _____

When _____

DATE NIGHT

What _____

Where _____

When _____

DATE NIGHT

What _____

Where _____

When _____

DATE NIGHT

What _____

Where _____

When _____

DATE NIGHT

What _____

Where _____

When _____

DATE NIGHT

What _____

Where _____

When _____

•••••••●●●●●♡●●●●●•••••

THINGS TO DO

Pickup

Calls

Sitter

THINGS TO DO

Pickup

Calls

Sitter

THINGS TO DO

Pickup

Calls

Sitter

MONTH _____

•••••●●●●♡●●●●••••

DATE NIGHT

What_____

Where_____

When_____

DATE NIGHT

What_____

Where_____

When_____

DATE NIGHT

What_____

Where_____

When_____

DATE NIGHT

What_____

Where_____

When_____

DATE NIGHT

What_____

Where_____

When_____

DATE NIGHT

What_____

Where_____

When_____

DATE NIGHT

What_____

Where_____

When_____

DATE NIGHT

What_____

Where_____

When_____

DATE NIGHT

What_____

Where_____

When_____

•••••●●●●♡●●●●••••

THINGS TO DO

Pickup

Calls

Sitter

THINGS TO DO

Pickup

Calls

Sitter

THINGS TO DO

Pickup

Calls

Sitter

MONTH _____

•••••●●●●♡●●●●●•••

DATE NIGHT

What _____

Where _____

When _____

DATE NIGHT

What _____

Where _____

When _____

DATE NIGHT

What _____

Where _____

When _____

DATE NIGHT

What _____

Where _____

When _____

DATE NIGHT

What _____

Where _____

When _____

DATE NIGHT

What _____

Where _____

When _____

DATE NIGHT

What _____

Where _____

When _____

DATE NIGHT

What _____

Where _____

When _____

DATE NIGHT

What _____

Where _____

When _____

•••••●●●●♡●●●●●•••

THINGS TO DO

Pickup

Calls

Sitter

THINGS TO DO

Pickup

Calls

Sitter

THINGS TO DO

Pickup

Calls

Sitter

MONTH _____

••••••●●●●❤●●●●••••

DATE NIGHT	DATE NIGHT	DATE NIGHT
What _____	What _____	What _____
Where _____	Where _____	Where _____
When _____	When _____	When _____

DATE NIGHT	DATE NIGHT	DATE NIGHT
What _____	What _____	What _____
Where _____	Where _____	Where _____
When _____	When _____	When _____

DATE NIGHT	DATE NIGHT	DATE NIGHT
What _____	What _____	What _____
Where _____	Where _____	Where _____
When _____	When _____	When _____

••••••●●●●❤●●●●••••

THINGS TO DO	THINGS TO DO	THINGS TO DO
Pickup	Pickup	Pickup
Calls	Calls	Calls
Sitter	Sitter	Sitter

MONTH _____

• • • • • • ● ● ● ● ● ● ♡ ● ● ● ● ● • • • •

DATE NIGHT	DATE NIGHT	DATE NIGHT
What _____	*What* _____	*What* _____
Where _____	*Where* _____	*Where* _____
When _____	*When* _____	*When* _____

DATE NIGHT	DATE NIGHT	DATE NIGHT
What _____	*What* _____	*What* _____
Where _____	*Where* _____	*Where* _____
When _____	*When* _____	*When* _____

DATE NIGHT	DATE NIGHT	DATE NIGHT
What _____	*What* _____	*What* _____
Where _____	*Where* _____	*Where* _____
When _____	*When* _____	*When* _____

• • • • • • ● ● ● ● ● ● ♡ ● ● ● ● ● • • • •

THINGS TO DO	THINGS TO DO	THINGS TO DO
Pickup	*Pickup*	*Pickup*
Calls	*Calls*	*Calls*
Sitter	*Sitter*	*Sitter*

MONTH _____

• • • • • • • ● ● ● ● ♡ ● ● ● ● • • • • •

DATE NIGHT

What_____

Where_____

When_____

DATE NIGHT

What_____

Where_____

When_____

DATE NIGHT

What_____

Where_____

When_____

DATE NIGHT

What_____

Where_____

When_____

DATE NIGHT

What_____

Where_____

When_____

DATE NIGHT

What_____

Where_____

When_____

DATE NIGHT

What_____

Where_____

When_____

DATE NIGHT

What_____

Where_____

When_____

DATE NIGHT

What_____

Where_____

When_____

• • • • • • ● ● ● ♡ ● ● ● ● • • • •

THINGS TO DO

Pickup

Calls

Sitter

THINGS TO DO

Pickup

Calls

Sitter

THINGS TO DO

Pickup

Calls

Sitter

MONTH _____

•••••••●●●●●♡●●●●•••••

DATE NIGHT	DATE NIGHT	DATE NIGHT
What _____	What _____	What _____
Where _____	Where _____	Where _____
When _____	When _____	When _____

DATE NIGHT	DATE NIGHT	DATE NIGHT
What _____	What _____	What _____
Where _____	Where _____	Where _____
When _____	When _____	When _____

DATE NIGHT	DATE NIGHT	DATE NIGHT
What _____	What _____	What _____
Where _____	Where _____	Where _____
When _____	When _____	When _____

•••••••●●●●●♡●●●●•••••

THINGS TO DO	THINGS TO DO	THINGS TO DO
Pickup	Pickup	Pickup
Calls	Calls	Calls
Sitter	Sitter	Sitter

MONTH _____

• • • • • • • • ● ♡ ● ● • • • • •

DATE NIGHT

What _____

Where _____

When _____

DATE NIGHT

What _____

Where _____

When _____

DATE NIGHT

What _____

Where _____

When _____

DATE NIGHT

What _____

Where _____

When _____

DATE NIGHT

What _____

Where _____

When _____

DATE NIGHT

What _____

Where _____

When _____

DATE NIGHT

What _____

Where _____

When _____

DATE NIGHT

What _____

Where _____

When _____

DATE NIGHT

What _____

Where _____

When _____

• • • • • • • ● ♡ ● ● • • • • •

THINGS TO DO

Pickup

Calls

Sitter

THINGS TO DO

Pickup

Calls

Sitter

THINGS TO DO

Pickup

Calls

Sitter

MONTH _____

• • • • • • • • ● ● ● ● ♡ ● ● ● ● • • • • •

DATE NIGHT

*What*_____

*Where*_____

*When*_____

DATE NIGHT

*What*_____

*Where*_____

*When*_____

DATE NIGHT

*What*_____

*Where*_____

*When*_____

DATE NIGHT

*What*_____

*Where*_____

*When*_____

DATE NIGHT

*What*_____

*Where*_____

*When*_____

DATE NIGHT

*What*_____

*Where*_____

*When*_____

DATE NIGHT

*What*_____

*Where*_____

*When*_____

DATE NIGHT

*What*_____

*Where*_____

*When*_____

DATE NIGHT

*What*_____

*Where*_____

*When*_____

• • • • • • • ● ● ● ● ♡ ● ● ● ● • • • • •

THINGS TO DO

Pickup

Calls

Sitter

THINGS TO DO

Pickup

Calls

Sitter

THINGS TO DO

Pickup

Calls

Sitter

MONTH _____

•••••●●●●●●●●♡●●●●●●••••

DATE NIGHT	DATE NIGHT	DATE NIGHT
What _____	*What* _____	*What* _____
Where _____	*Where* _____	*Where* _____
When _____	*When* _____	*When* _____

DATE NIGHT	DATE NIGHT	DATE NIGHT
What _____	*What* _____	*What* _____
Where _____	*Where* _____	*Where* _____
When _____	*When* _____	*When* _____

DATE NIGHT	DATE NIGHT	DATE NIGHT
What _____	*What* _____	*What* _____
Where _____	*Where* _____	*Where* _____
When _____	*When* _____	*When* _____

•••••●●●●●●●♡●●●●●●●••••

THINGS TO DO	THINGS TO DO	THINGS TO DO
Pickup	*Pickup*	*Pickup*
Calls	*Calls*	*Calls*
Sitter	*Sitter*	*Sitter*

MONTH _____

•••••••●●●●♡●●●●••••

DATE NIGHT	DATE NIGHT	DATE NIGHT
What _____	*What* _____	*What* _____
Where _____	*Where* _____	*Where* _____
When _____	*When* _____	*When* _____

DATE NIGHT	DATE NIGHT	DATE NIGHT
What _____	*What* _____	*What* _____
Where _____	*Where* _____	*Where* _____
When _____	*When* _____	*When* _____

DATE NIGHT	DATE NIGHT	DATE NIGHT
What _____	*What* _____	*What* _____
Where _____	*Where* _____	*Where* _____
When _____	*When* _____	*When* _____

•••••••●●●●♡●●●●••••

THINGS TO DO   THINGS TO DO   THINGS TO DO

Pickup   *Pickup*   *Pickup*

Calls   *Calls*   *Calls*

Sitter   *Sitter*   *Sitter*

MONTH _____

•••••••• ● ● ● ● ♡ ● ● ● ●•••••••

DATE NIGHT	DATE NIGHT	DATE NIGHT
What _____	What _____	What _____
Where _____	Where _____	Where _____
When _____	When _____	When _____

DATE NIGHT	DATE NIGHT	DATE NIGHT
What _____	What _____	What _____
Where _____	Where _____	Where _____
When _____	When _____	When _____

DATE NIGHT	DATE NIGHT	DATE NIGHT
What _____	What _____	What _____
Where _____	Where _____	Where _____
When _____	When _____	When _____

•••••••• ● ● ● ● ♡ ● ● ● ●•••••••

THINGS TO DO	THINGS TO DO	THINGS TO DO
Pickup	Pickup	Pickup
Calls	Calls	Calls
Sitter	Sitter	Sitter

MONTH _____

•••••••••●●●♡●●●●•••••

DATE NIGHT

What _____

Where _____

When _____

DATE NIGHT

What _____

Where _____

When _____

DATE NIGHT

What _____

Where _____

When _____

DATE NIGHT

What _____

Where _____

When _____

DATE NIGHT

What _____

Where _____

When _____

DATE NIGHT

What _____

Where _____

When _____

DATE NIGHT

What _____

Where _____

When _____

DATE NIGHT

What _____

Where _____

When _____

DATE NIGHT

What _____

Where _____

When _____

•••••••●●●♡●●●••••••

THINGS TO DO

Pickup

Calls

Sitter

THINGS TO DO

Pickup

Calls

Sitter

THINGS TO DO

Pickup

Calls

Sitter

MONTH _____

•••••••●●●●♡●●●●••••

DATE NIGHT

What _____

Where _____

When _____

DATE NIGHT

What _____

Where _____

When _____

DATE NIGHT

What _____

Where _____

When _____

DATE NIGHT

What _____

Where _____

When _____

DATE NIGHT

What _____

Where _____

When _____

DATE NIGHT

What _____

Where _____

When _____

DATE NIGHT

What _____

Where _____

When _____

DATE NIGHT

What _____

Where _____

When _____

DATE NIGHT

What _____

Where _____

When _____

•••••••●●●●♡●●●●••••

THINGS TO DO

Pickup

Calls

Sitter

THINGS TO DO

Pickup

Calls

Sitter

THINGS TO DO

Pickup

Calls

Sitter

MONTH _____

•••••••●●●●●♡●●●●•••••

DATE NIGHT

*What*_____

*Where*_____

*When*_____

DATE NIGHT

*What*_____

*Where*_____

*When*_____

DATE NIGHT

*What*_____

*Where*_____

*When*_____

DATE NIGHT

*What*_____

*Where*_____

*When*_____

DATE NIGHT

*What*_____

*Where*_____

*When*_____

DATE NIGHT

*What*_____

*Where*_____

*When*_____

DATE NIGHT

*What*_____

*Where*_____

*When*_____

DATE NIGHT

*What*_____

*Where*_____

*When*_____

DATE NIGHT

*What*_____

*Where*_____

*When*_____

•••••••●●●●●♡●●●●•••••

THINGS TO DO

Pickup

Calls

Sitter

THINGS TO DO

Pickup

Calls

Sitter

THINGS TO DO

Pickup

Calls

Sitter

MONTH _____

•••••●●●●●♡●●●●●•••••

DATE NIGHT

What _____

Where _____

When _____

DATE NIGHT

What _____

Where _____

When _____

DATE NIGHT

What _____

Where _____

When _____

DATE NIGHT

What _____

Where _____

When _____

DATE NIGHT

What _____

Where _____

When _____

DATE NIGHT

What _____

Where _____

When _____

DATE NIGHT

What _____

Where _____

When _____

DATE NIGHT

What _____

Where _____

When _____

DATE NIGHT

What _____

Where _____

When _____

•••••●●●●●♡●●●●●•••••

THINGS TO DO

Pickup

Calls

Sitter

THINGS TO DO

Pickup

Calls

Sitter

THINGS TO DO

Pickup

Calls

Sitter

MONTH _____

•••••●●●●●♡●●●●●●•••

DATE NIGHT	DATE NIGHT	DATE NIGHT
What _____	What _____	What _____
Where _____	Where _____	Where _____
When _____	When _____	When _____

DATE NIGHT	DATE NIGHT	DATE NIGHT
What _____	What _____	What _____
Where _____	Where _____	Where _____
When _____	When _____	When _____

DATE NIGHT	DATE NIGHT	DATE NIGHT
What _____	What _____	What _____
Where _____	Where _____	Where _____
When _____	When _____	When _____

•••••●●●●●♡●●●●●●•••

THINGS TO DO	THINGS TO DO	THINGS TO DO
Pickup	Pickup	Pickup
Calls	Calls	Calls
Sitter	Sitter	Sitter

MONTH _____

•••••••••••••••••♡•••••••••••••••

DATE NIGHT

What_____

Where_____

When_____

DATE NIGHT

What_____

Where_____

When_____

DATE NIGHT

What_____

Where_____

When_____

DATE NIGHT

What_____

Where_____

When_____

DATE NIGHT

What_____

Where_____

When_____

DATE NIGHT

What_____

Where_____

When_____

DATE NIGHT

What_____

Where_____

When_____

DATE NIGHT

What_____

Where_____

When_____

DATE NIGHT

What_____

Where_____

When_____

•••••••••••••♡•••••••••••••

THINGS TO DO

Pickup

Calls

Sitter

THINGS TO DO

Pickup

Calls

Sitter

THINGS TO DO

Pickup

Calls

Sitter

MONTH _____

•••••●●●●●♡●●●●●•••••

DATE NIGHT

What _____

Where _____

When _____

DATE NIGHT

What _____

Where _____

When _____

DATE NIGHT

What _____

Where _____

When _____

DATE NIGHT

What _____

Where _____

When _____

DATE NIGHT

What _____

Where _____

When _____

DATE NIGHT

What _____

Where _____

When _____

DATE NIGHT

What _____

Where _____

When _____

DATE NIGHT

What _____

Where _____

When _____

DATE NIGHT

What _____

Where _____

When _____

•••••●●●●●♡●●●●●•••••

THINGS TO DO

Pickup

Calls

Sitter

THINGS TO DO

Pickup

Calls

Sitter

THINGS TO DO

Pickup

Calls

Sitter

MONTH _____

• • • • • • ● ● ● ♡ ● ● ● ● • • • •

DATE NIGHT	DATE NIGHT	DATE NIGHT
What _____	What _____	What _____
Where _____	Where _____	Where _____
When _____	When _____	When _____

DATE NIGHT	DATE NIGHT	DATE NIGHT
What _____	What _____	What _____
Where _____	Where _____	Where _____
When _____	When _____	When _____

DATE NIGHT	DATE NIGHT	DATE NIGHT
What _____	What _____	What _____
Where _____	Where _____	Where _____
When _____	When _____	When _____

• • • • • ● ● ● ♡ ● ● ● • • • • •

THINGS TO DO	THINGS TO DO	THINGS TO DO
Pickup	Pickup	Pickup
Calls	Calls	Calls
Sitter	Sitter	Sitter

MONTH _____

•••••••●●●●♡●●●●•••••

DATE NIGHT

What _____

Where _____

When _____

DATE NIGHT

What _____

Where _____

When _____

DATE NIGHT

What _____

Where _____

When _____

DATE NIGHT

What _____

Where _____

When _____

DATE NIGHT

What _____

Where _____

When _____

DATE NIGHT

What _____

Where _____

When _____

DATE NIGHT

What _____

Where _____

When _____

DATE NIGHT

What _____

Where _____

When _____

DATE NIGHT

What _____

Where _____

When _____

•••••••●●●●♡●●●●•••••

THINGS TO DO

Pickup

Calls

Sitter

THINGS TO DO

Pickup

Calls

Sitter

THINGS TO DO

Pickup

Calls

Sitter

MONTH _____

• • • • • • ● ● ● ● ● ♡ ● ● ● ● ● • • • •

DATE NIGHT	DATE NIGHT	DATE NIGHT
What _____	*What* _____	*What* _____
Where _____	*Where* _____	*Where* _____
When _____	*When* _____	*When* _____

DATE NIGHT	DATE NIGHT	DATE NIGHT
What _____	*What* _____	*What* _____
Where _____	*Where* _____	*Where* _____
When _____	*When* _____	*When* _____

DATE NIGHT	DATE NIGHT	DATE NIGHT
What _____	*What* _____	*What* _____
Where _____	*Where* _____	*Where* _____
When _____	*When* _____	*When* _____

• • • • • • ● ● ● ● ● ♡ ● ● ● ● ● • • • •

THINGS TO DO	THINGS TO DO	THINGS TO DO
Pickup	*Pickup*	*Pickup*
Calls	*Calls*	*Calls*
Sitter	*Sitter*	*Sitter*

MONTH _____

••••●●●●●♡●●●●•••

DATE NIGHT

What _____

Where _____

When _____

DATE NIGHT

What _____

Where _____

When _____

DATE NIGHT

What _____

Where _____

When _____

DATE NIGHT

What _____

Where _____

When _____

DATE NIGHT

What _____

Where _____

When _____

DATE NIGHT

What _____

Where _____

When _____

DATE NIGHT

What _____

Where _____

When _____

DATE NIGHT

What _____

Where _____

When _____

DATE NIGHT

What _____

Where _____

When _____

••••●●●●●♡●●●●•••

THINGS TO DO

Pickup

Calls

Sitter

THINGS TO DO

Pickup

Calls

Sitter

THINGS TO DO

Pickup

Calls

Sitter

MONTH _____

•••••●●●●♡●●●●•••

DATE NIGHT

What _____

Where _____

When _____

DATE NIGHT

What _____

Where _____

When _____

DATE NIGHT

What _____

Where _____

When _____

DATE NIGHT

What _____

Where _____

When _____

DATE NIGHT

What _____

Where _____

When _____

DATE NIGHT

What _____

Where _____

When _____

DATE NIGHT

What _____

Where _____

When _____

DATE NIGHT

What _____

Where _____

When _____

DATE NIGHT

What _____

Where _____

When _____

•••••●●●●♡●●●●•••

THINGS TO DO

Pickup

Calls

Sitter

THINGS TO DO

Pickup

Calls

Sitter

THINGS TO DO

Pickup

Calls

Sitter

MONTH _____

• • • • • ● ● ● ● ● ● ♡ ● ● ● ● ● • • • •

DATE NIGHT

What _____

Where _____

When _____

DATE NIGHT

What _____

Where _____

When _____

DATE NIGHT

What _____

Where _____

When _____

DATE NIGHT

What _____

Where _____

When _____

DATE NIGHT

What _____

Where _____

When _____

DATE NIGHT

What _____

Where _____

When _____

DATE NIGHT

What _____

Where _____

When _____

DATE NIGHT

What _____

Where _____

When _____

DATE NIGHT

What _____

Where _____

When _____

• • • • • ● ● ● ● ● ● ♡ ● ● ● ● ● • • • •

THINGS TO DO

Pickup

Calls

Sitter

THINGS TO DO

Pickup

Calls

Sitter

THINGS TO DO

Pickup

Calls

Sitter

MONTH _____

•••••●●●●●♡●●●●••••

DATE NIGHT	DATE NIGHT	DATE NIGHT
*What*_____	*What*_____	*What*_____
*Where*_____	*Where*_____	*Where*_____
*When*_____	*When*_____	*When*_____

DATE NIGHT	DATE NIGHT	DATE NIGHT
*What*_____	*What*_____	*What*_____
*Where*_____	*Where*_____	*Where*_____
*When*_____	*When*_____	*When*_____

DATE NIGHT	DATE NIGHT	DATE NIGHT
*What*_____	*What*_____	*What*_____
*Where*_____	*Where*_____	*Where*_____
*When*_____	*When*_____	*When*_____

•••••●●●●●♡●●●●••••

THINGS TO DO	THINGS TO DO	THINGS TO DO
Pickup	*Pickup*	*Pickup*
Calls	*Calls*	*Calls*
Sitter	*Sitter*	*Sitter*

MONTH _____

•••••••●●●●●♡●●●●•••••

DATE NIGHT	DATE NIGHT	DATE NIGHT
What _____	*What* _____	*What* _____
Where _____	*Where* _____	*Where* _____
When _____	*When* _____	*When* _____

DATE NIGHT	DATE NIGHT	DATE NIGHT
What _____	*What* _____	*What* _____
Where _____	*Where* _____	*Where* _____
When _____	*When* _____	*When* _____

DATE NIGHT	DATE NIGHT	DATE NIGHT
What _____	*What* _____	*What* _____
Where _____	*Where* _____	*Where* _____
When _____	*When* _____	*When* _____

•••••••●●●●♡●●●●●•••••

THINGS TO DO	THINGS TO DO	THINGS TO DO
Pickup	*Pickup*	*Pickup*
Calls	*Calls*	*Calls*
Sitter	*Sitter*	*Sitter*

MONTH _____

• • • • • • • • • ● ● ● ♡ ● ● ● ● • • • • •

DATE NIGHT	DATE NIGHT	DATE NIGHT
What _____	*What* _____	*What* _____
Where _____	*Where* _____	*Where* _____
When _____	*When* _____	*When* _____

DATE NIGHT	DATE NIGHT	DATE NIGHT
What _____	*What* _____	*What* _____
Where _____	*Where* _____	*Where* _____
When _____	*When* _____	*When* _____

DATE NIGHT	DATE NIGHT	DATE NIGHT
What _____	*What* _____	*What* _____
Where _____	*Where* _____	*Where* _____
When _____	*When* _____	*When* _____

• • • • • • • • ● ● ● ♡ ● ● ● • • • • • •

THINGS TO DO	THINGS TO DO	THINGS TO DO
Pickup	*Pickup*	*Pickup*
Calls	*Calls*	*Calls*
Sitter	*Sitter*	*Sitter*

MONTH _____

● ● ● ● ● ● ● ● ● ♡ ● ● ● ● ● ● ●

DATE NIGHT	DATE NIGHT	DATE NIGHT
What_____	What_____	What_____
Where_____	Where_____	Where_____
When_____	When_____	When_____

DATE NIGHT	DATE NIGHT	DATE NIGHT
What_____	What_____	What_____
Where_____	Where_____	Where_____
When_____	When_____	When_____

DATE NIGHT	DATE NIGHT	DATE NIGHT
What_____	What_____	What_____
Where_____	Where_____	Where_____
When_____	When_____	When_____

● ● ● ● ● ● ● ● ● ♡ ● ● ● ● ● ● ●

THINGS TO DO	THINGS TO DO	THINGS TO DO
Pickup	Pickup	Pickup
Calls	Calls	Calls
Sitter	Sitter	Sitter

MONTH _____

•••••●●●●♡●●●●•••••

DATE NIGHT

What_____

Where_____

When_____

DATE NIGHT

What_____

Where_____

When_____

DATE NIGHT

What_____

Where_____

When_____

DATE NIGHT

What_____

Where_____

When_____

DATE NIGHT

What_____

Where_____

When_____

DATE NIGHT

What_____

Where_____

When_____

DATE NIGHT

What_____

Where_____

When_____

DATE NIGHT

What_____

Where_____

When_____

DATE NIGHT

What_____

Where_____

When_____

•••••●●●●♡●●●●•••••

THINGS TO DO

Pickup

Calls

Sitter

THINGS TO DO

Pickup

Calls

Sitter

THINGS TO DO

Pickup

Calls

Sitter

MONTH _____

•••••••●●●●●●♡●●●●●•••••

DATE NIGHT	DATE NIGHT	DATE NIGHT
What _____	*What* _____	*What* _____
Where _____	*Where* _____	*Where* _____
When _____	*When* _____	*When* _____

DATE NIGHT	DATE NIGHT	DATE NIGHT
What _____	*What* _____	*What* _____
Where _____	*Where* _____	*Where* _____
When _____	*When* _____	*When* _____

DATE NIGHT	DATE NIGHT	DATE NIGHT
What _____	*What* _____	*What* _____
Where _____	*Where* _____	*Where* _____
When _____	*When* _____	*When* _____

•••••••●●●●●●♡●●●●●•••••

THINGS TO DO	THINGS TO DO	THINGS TO DO
Pickup	*Pickup*	*Pickup*
Calls	*Calls*	*Calls*
Sitter	*Sitter*	*Sitter*

MONTH _____

•••••••••●●●●●○●●●●●••••••

DATE NIGHT

What_____

Where_____

When_____

DATE NIGHT

What_____

Where_____

When_____

DATE NIGHT

What_____

Where_____

When_____

DATE NIGHT

What_____

Where_____

When_____

DATE NIGHT

What_____

Where_____

When_____

DATE NIGHT

What_____

Where_____

When_____

DATE NIGHT

What_____

Where_____

When_____

DATE NIGHT

What_____

Where_____

When_____

DATE NIGHT

What_____

Where_____

When_____

•••••••••●●●●●○●●●●●••••••

THINGS TO DO

Pickup

Calls

Sitter

THINGS TO DO

Pickup

Calls

Sitter

THINGS TO DO

Pickup

Calls

Sitter

MONTH _____

•••••●●●●●●◯●●●●●●•••••

DATE NIGHT

What _____

Where _____

When _____

DATE NIGHT

What _____

Where _____

When _____

DATE NIGHT

What _____

Where _____

When _____

DATE NIGHT

What _____

Where _____

When _____

DATE NIGHT

What _____

Where _____

When _____

DATE NIGHT

What _____

Where _____

When _____

DATE NIGHT

What _____

Where _____

When _____

DATE NIGHT

What _____

Where _____

When _____

DATE NIGHT

What _____

Where _____

When _____

•••••●●●●●●◯●●●●●●•••••

THINGS TO DO

Pickup

Calls

Sitter

THINGS TO DO

Pickup

Calls

Sitter

THINGS TO DO

Pickup

Calls

Sitter

MONTH _____

•••••••●●●●●♡●●●●●●•••

DATE NIGHT

What_____

Where_____

When_____

DATE NIGHT

What_____

Where_____

When_____

DATE NIGHT

What_____

Where_____

When_____

DATE NIGHT

What_____

Where_____

When_____

DATE NIGHT

What_____

Where_____

When_____

DATE NIGHT

What_____

Where_____

When_____

DATE NIGHT

What_____

Where_____

When_____

DATE NIGHT

What_____

Where_____

When_____

DATE NIGHT

What_____

Where_____

When_____

•••••••●●●●●♡●●●●●●•••

THINGS TO DO

Pickup

Calls

Sitter

THINGS TO DO

Pickup

Calls

Sitter

THINGS TO DO

Pickup

Calls

Sitter

MONTH _____

•••••●●●●●●●♡●●●●●●•••

DATE NIGHT	DATE NIGHT	DATE NIGHT
What _____	What _____	What _____
Where _____	Where _____	Where _____
When _____	When _____	When _____

DATE NIGHT	DATE NIGHT	DATE NIGHT
What _____	What _____	What _____
Where _____	Where _____	Where _____
When _____	When _____	When _____

DATE NIGHT	DATE NIGHT	DATE NIGHT
What _____	What _____	What _____
Where _____	Where _____	Where _____
When _____	When _____	When _____

•••••●●●●●●♡●●●●●•••

THINGS TO DO	THINGS TO DO	THINGS TO DO
Pickup	Pickup	Pickup
Calls	Calls	Calls
Sitter	Sitter	Sitter

MONTH _____

•••••●●●●♡●●●●•••

DATE NIGHT

What _____

Where _____

When _____

DATE NIGHT

What _____

Where _____

When _____

DATE NIGHT

What _____

Where _____

When _____

DATE NIGHT

What _____

Where _____

When _____

DATE NIGHT

What _____

Where _____

When _____

DATE NIGHT

What _____

Where _____

When _____

DATE NIGHT

What _____

Where _____

When _____

DATE NIGHT

What _____

Where _____

When _____

DATE NIGHT

What _____

Where _____

When _____

•••••●●●●♡●●●●•••

THINGS TO DO

Pickup

Calls

Sitter

THINGS TO DO

Pickup

Calls

Sitter

THINGS TO DO

Pickup

Calls

Sitter

MONTH _____

•••••●●●●○●●●●•••••

DATE NIGHT	DATE NIGHT	DATE NIGHT
What _____	*What* _____	*What* _____
Where _____	*Where* _____	*Where* _____
When _____	*When* _____	*When* _____

DATE NIGHT	DATE NIGHT	DATE NIGHT
What _____	*What* _____	*What* _____
Where _____	*Where* _____	*Where* _____
When _____	*When* _____	*When* _____

DATE NIGHT	DATE NIGHT	DATE NIGHT
What _____	*What* _____	*What* _____
Where _____	*Where* _____	*Where* _____
When _____	*When* _____	*When* _____

•••••●●●●○●●●●•••••

THINGS TO DO	THINGS TO DO	THINGS TO DO
Pickup	*Pickup*	*Pickup*
Calls	*Calls*	*Calls*
Sitter	*Sitter*	*Sitter*

MONTH _____

•••••••●●●●●♡●●●●●●••••

DATE NIGHT

What _____

Where _____

When _____

DATE NIGHT

What _____

Where _____

When _____

DATE NIGHT

What _____

Where _____

When _____

DATE NIGHT

What _____

Where _____

When _____

DATE NIGHT

What _____

Where _____

When _____

DATE NIGHT

What _____

Where _____

When _____

DATE NIGHT

What _____

Where _____

When _____

DATE NIGHT

What _____

Where _____

When _____

DATE NIGHT

What _____

Where _____

When _____

••••••●●●●●♡●●●●●••••

THINGS TO DO

Pickup

Calls

Sitter

THINGS TO DO

Pickup

Calls

Sitter

THINGS TO DO

Pickup

Calls

Sitter

MONTH _____

•••••••●●●●♡●●●●•••••

DATE NIGHT	DATE NIGHT	DATE NIGHT
What _____	What _____	What _____
Where _____	Where _____	Where _____
When _____	When _____	When _____

DATE NIGHT	DATE NIGHT	DATE NIGHT
What _____	What _____	What _____
Where _____	Where _____	Where _____
When _____	When _____	When _____

DATE NIGHT	DATE NIGHT	DATE NIGHT
What _____	What _____	What _____
Where _____	Where _____	Where _____
When _____	When _____	When _____

•••••••●●●●♡●●●●•••••

THINGS TO DO	THINGS TO DO	THINGS TO DO
Pickup	Pickup	Pickup
Calls	Calls	Calls
Sitter	Sitter	Sitter

MONTH _____

•••••••●●●●●♡●●●●•••••••

DATE NIGHT	DATE NIGHT	DATE NIGHT
What _____	What _____	What _____
Where _____	Where _____	Where _____
When _____	When _____	When _____

DATE NIGHT	DATE NIGHT	DATE NIGHT
What _____	What _____	What _____
Where _____	Where _____	Where _____
When _____	When _____	When _____

DATE NIGHT	DATE NIGHT	DATE NIGHT
What _____	What _____	What _____
Where _____	Where _____	Where _____
When _____	When _____	When _____

•••••••●●●●●♡●●●●•••••••

THINGS TO DO	THINGS TO DO	THINGS TO DO
Pickup	Pickup	Pickup
Calls	Calls	Calls
Sitter	Sitter	Sitter

MONTH _____

•••••●●●●●●♡●●●●●●••••

DATE NIGHT	DATE NIGHT	DATE NIGHT
What _____	*What* _____	*What* _____
Where _____	*Where* _____	*Where* _____
When _____	*When* _____	*When* _____

DATE NIGHT	DATE NIGHT	DATE NIGHT
What _____	*What* _____	*What* _____
Where _____	*Where* _____	*Where* _____
When _____	*When* _____	*When* _____

DATE NIGHT	DATE NIGHT	DATE NIGHT
What _____	*What* _____	*What* _____
Where _____	*Where* _____	*Where* _____
When _____	*When* _____	*When* _____

•••••●●●●●●♡●●●●●●••••

THINGS TO DO	THINGS TO DO	THINGS TO DO
Pickup	*Pickup*	*Pickup*
Calls	*Calls*	*Calls*
Sitter	*Sitter*	*Sitter*

MONTH _____

•••••●●●●●♡●●●●•••••

DATE NIGHT

What_____

Where_____

When_____

DATE NIGHT

What_____

Where_____

When_____

DATE NIGHT

What_____

Where_____

When_____

DATE NIGHT

What_____

Where_____

When_____

DATE NIGHT

What_____

Where_____

When_____

DATE NIGHT

What_____

Where_____

When_____

DATE NIGHT

What_____

Where_____

When_____

DATE NIGHT

What_____

Where_____

When_____

DATE NIGHT

What_____

Where_____

When_____

•••••●●●●●♡●●●●•••••

THINGS TO DO

Pickup

Calls

Sitter

THINGS TO DO

Pickup

Calls

Sitter

THINGS TO DO

Pickup

Calls

Sitter

MONTH _____

•••••••••●●●●●●♡●●●●●•••••

DATE NIGHT

What _____

Where _____

When _____

DATE NIGHT

What _____

Where _____

When _____

DATE NIGHT

What _____

Where _____

When _____

DATE NIGHT

What _____

Where _____

When _____

DATE NIGHT

What _____

Where _____

When _____

DATE NIGHT

What _____

Where _____

When _____

DATE NIGHT

What _____

Where _____

When _____

DATE NIGHT

What _____

Where _____

When _____

DATE NIGHT

What _____

Where _____

When _____

•••••••••●●●●●●♡●●●●●•••••

THINGS TO DO

Pickup

Calls

Sitter

THINGS TO DO

Pickup

Calls

Sitter

THINGS TO DO

Pickup

Calls

Sitter

MONTH _____

●●●●●●●●●●♡●●●●●●●●

DATE NIGHT

What_____

Where_____

When_____

DATE NIGHT

What_____

Where_____

When_____

DATE NIGHT

What_____

Where_____

When_____

DATE NIGHT

What_____

Where_____

When_____

DATE NIGHT

What_____

Where_____

When_____

DATE NIGHT

What_____

Where_____

When_____

DATE NIGHT

What_____

Where_____

When_____

DATE NIGHT

What_____

Where_____

When_____

DATE NIGHT

What_____

Where_____

When_____

●●●●●●●●●●♡●●●●●●●●

THINGS TO DO

Pickup

Calls

Sitter

THINGS TO DO

Pickup

Calls

Sitter

THINGS TO DO

Pickup

Calls

Sitter

MONTH _____

•••••••● ● ● ● ● ♡ ● ● ● ● •••••

DATE NIGHT

What _____

Where _____

When _____

DATE NIGHT

What _____

Where _____

When _____

DATE NIGHT

What _____

Where _____

When _____

DATE NIGHT

What _____

Where _____

When _____

DATE NIGHT

What _____

Where _____

When _____

DATE NIGHT

What _____

Where _____

When _____

DATE NIGHT

What _____

Where _____

When _____

DATE NIGHT

What _____

Where _____

When _____

DATE NIGHT

What _____

Where _____

When _____

•••••••● ● ● ● ● ♡ ● ● ● ● •••••

THINGS TO DO

Pickup

Calls

Sitter

THINGS TO DO

Pickup

Calls

Sitter

THINGS TO DO

Pickup

Calls

Sitter

MONTH _____

• • • • • • • • ● ● ● ● ● ♡ ● ● ● ● • • • • • •

DATE NIGHT

What_____

Where_____

When_____

DATE NIGHT

What_____

Where_____

When_____

DATE NIGHT

What_____

Where_____

When_____

DATE NIGHT

What_____

Where_____

When_____

DATE NIGHT

What_____

Where_____

When_____

DATE NIGHT

What_____

Where_____

When_____

DATE NIGHT

What_____

Where_____

When_____

DATE NIGHT

What_____

Where_____

When_____

DATE NIGHT

What_____

Where_____

When_____

• • • • • • • • ● ● ● ● ● ♡ ● ● ● ● • • • • • •

THINGS TO DO

Pickup

Calls

Sitter

THINGS TO DO

Pickup

Calls

Sitter

THINGS TO DO

Pickup

Calls

Sitter

MONTH _____

•••••••●●●●●♡●●●●●•••••

DATE NIGHT	DATE NIGHT	DATE NIGHT
What _____	What _____	What _____
Where _____	Where _____	Where _____
When _____	When _____	When _____

DATE NIGHT	DATE NIGHT	DATE NIGHT
What _____	What _____	What _____
Where _____	Where _____	Where _____
When _____	When _____	When _____

DATE NIGHT	DATE NIGHT	DATE NIGHT
What _____	What _____	What _____
Where _____	Where _____	Where _____
When _____	When _____	When _____

•••••••●●●●♡●●●●●•••••

THINGS TO DO	THINGS TO DO	THINGS TO DO
Pickup	Pickup	Pickup
Calls	Calls	Calls
Sitter	Sitter	Sitter

MONTH _____

••••••●●●●●♡●●●●●••••

DATE NIGHT	DATE NIGHT	DATE NIGHT
What _____	What _____	What _____
Where _____	Where _____	Where _____
When _____	When _____	When _____

DATE NIGHT	DATE NIGHT	DATE NIGHT
What _____	What _____	What _____
Where _____	Where _____	Where _____
When _____	When _____	When _____

DATE NIGHT	DATE NIGHT	DATE NIGHT
What _____	What _____	What _____
Where _____	Where _____	Where _____
When _____	When _____	When _____

••••••●●●●♡●●●●••••

THINGS TO DO	THINGS TO DO	THINGS TO DO
Pickup	Pickup	Pickup
Calls	Calls	Calls
Sitter	Sitter	Sitter

MONTH _____

• • • • • • • • ● ● ● ♡ ● ● ● ● • • • • •

DATE NIGHT	DATE NIGHT	DATE NIGHT
What_____	What_____	What_____
Where_____	Where_____	Where_____
When_____	When_____	When_____

DATE NIGHT	DATE NIGHT	DATE NIGHT
What_____	What_____	What_____
Where_____	Where_____	Where_____
When_____	When_____	When_____

DATE NIGHT	DATE NIGHT	DATE NIGHT
What_____	What_____	What_____
Where_____	Where_____	Where_____
When_____	When_____	When_____

• • • • • • • • ● ● ● ♡ ● ● ● ● • • • • •

THINGS TO DO	THINGS TO DO	THINGS TO DO
Pickup	Pickup	Pickup
Calls	Calls	Calls
Sitter	Sitter	Sitter

MONTH _____

· · · · · · ● ● ● ● ● ● ♡ ● ● ● ● ● · · · · ·

DATE NIGHT	DATE NIGHT	DATE NIGHT
What _____	*What* _____	*What* _____
Where _____	*Where* _____	*Where* _____
When _____	*When* _____	*When* _____

DATE NIGHT	DATE NIGHT	DATE NIGHT
What _____	*What* _____	*What* _____
Where _____	*Where* _____	*Where* _____
When _____	*When* _____	*When* _____

DATE NIGHT	DATE NIGHT	DATE NIGHT
What _____	*What* _____	*What* _____
Where _____	*Where* _____	*Where* _____
When _____	*When* _____	*When* _____

· · · · · · ● ● ● ● ● ♡ ● ● ● ● ● ● · · · · ·

THINGS TO DO	THINGS TO DO	THINGS TO DO
Pickup	*Pickup*	*Pickup*
Calls	*Calls*	*Calls*
Sitter	*Sitter*	*Sitter*

MONTH _____

•••••••••●●●●●♡●●●●••••••

DATE NIGHT	DATE NIGHT	DATE NIGHT
*What*_____	*What*_____	*What*_____
*Where*_____	*Where*_____	*Where*_____
*When*_____	*When*_____	*When*_____

DATE NIGHT	DATE NIGHT	DATE NIGHT
*What*_____	*What*_____	*What*_____
*Where*_____	*Where*_____	*Where*_____
*When*_____	*When*_____	*When*_____

DATE NIGHT	DATE NIGHT	DATE NIGHT
*What*_____	*What*_____	*What*_____
*Where*_____	*Where*_____	*Where*_____
*When*_____	*When*_____	*When*_____

•••••••••●●●●●♡●●●●••••••

THINGS TO DO	THINGS TO DO	THINGS TO DO
Pickup	*Pickup*	*Pickup*
Calls	*Calls*	*Calls*
Sitter	*Sitter*	*Sitter*

MONTH _____

•••••••●●●●●♡●●●●●•••••

DATE NIGHT

What_____

Where_____

When_____

DATE NIGHT

What_____

Where_____

When_____

DATE NIGHT

What_____

Where_____

When_____

DATE NIGHT

What_____

Where_____

When_____

DATE NIGHT

What_____

Where_____

When_____

DATE NIGHT

What_____

Where_____

When_____

DATE NIGHT

What_____

Where_____

When_____

DATE NIGHT

What_____

Where_____

When_____

DATE NIGHT

What_____

Where_____

When_____

•••••••●●●●●♡●●●●●•••••

THINGS TO DO

Pickup

Calls

Sitter

THINGS TO DO

Pickup

Calls

Sitter

THINGS TO DO

Pickup

Calls

Sitter

MONTH _____

•••••••●●●●●♡●●●●•••••

DATE NIGHT

What_____

Where_____

When_____

DATE NIGHT

What_____

Where_____

When_____

DATE NIGHT

What_____

Where_____

When_____

DATE NIGHT

What_____

Where_____

When_____

DATE NIGHT

What_____

Where_____

When_____

DATE NIGHT

What_____

Where_____

When_____

DATE NIGHT

What_____

Where_____

When_____

DATE NIGHT

What_____

Where_____

When_____

DATE NIGHT

What_____

Where_____

When_____

•••••••●●●●●♡●●●●•••••

THINGS TO DO

Pickup

Calls

Sitter

THINGS TO DO

Pickup

Calls

Sitter

THINGS TO DO

Pickup

Calls

Sitter

MONTH _____

•••••••●●●●●♡●●●●●•••••

DATE NIGHT

What _____

Where _____

When _____

DATE NIGHT

What _____

Where _____

When _____

DATE NIGHT

What _____

Where _____

When _____

DATE NIGHT

What _____

Where _____

When _____

DATE NIGHT

What _____

Where _____

When _____

DATE NIGHT

What _____

Where _____

When _____

DATE NIGHT

What _____

Where _____

When _____

DATE NIGHT

What _____

Where _____

When _____

DATE NIGHT

What _____

Where _____

When _____

•••••••●●●●●♡●●●●●•••••

THINGS TO DO

Pickup

Calls

Sitter

THINGS TO DO

Pickup

Calls

Sitter

THINGS TO DO

Pickup

Calls

Sitter

MONTH _____

• • • • • • • • • ♡ • • • • • • • •

DATE NIGHT

What _____

Where _____

When _____

DATE NIGHT

What _____

Where _____

When _____

DATE NIGHT

What _____

Where _____

When _____

DATE NIGHT

What _____

Where _____

When _____

DATE NIGHT

What _____

Where _____

When _____

DATE NIGHT

What _____

Where _____

When _____

DATE NIGHT

What _____

Where _____

When _____

DATE NIGHT

What _____

Where _____

When _____

DATE NIGHT

What _____

Where _____

When _____

• • • • • • • • ♡ • • • • • • • •

THINGS TO DO

Pickup

Calls

Sitter

THINGS TO DO

Pickup

Calls

Sitter

THINGS TO DO

Pickup

Calls

Sitter

MONTH _____

•••••••●●●●♡●●●●•••••

DATE NIGHT	DATE NIGHT	DATE NIGHT
*What*_____	*What*_____	*What*_____
*Where*_____	*Where*_____	*Where*_____
*When*_____	*When*_____	*When*_____

DATE NIGHT	DATE NIGHT	DATE NIGHT
*What*_____	*What*_____	*What*_____
*Where*_____	*Where*_____	*Where*_____
*When*_____	*When*_____	*When*_____

DATE NIGHT	DATE NIGHT	DATE NIGHT
*What*_____	*What*_____	*What*_____
*Where*_____	*Where*_____	*Where*_____
*When*_____	*When*_____	*When*_____

•••••••●●●●♡●●●●•••••

THINGS TO DO	THINGS TO DO	THINGS TO DO
Pickup	*Pickup*	*Pickup*
Calls	*Calls*	*Calls*
Sitter	*Sitter*	*Sitter*

MONTH _____

• • • • • • • ● ● ● ● ♡ ● ● ● ● • • • • •

DATE NIGHT

What_____

Where_____

When_____

DATE NIGHT

What_____

Where_____

When_____

DATE NIGHT

What_____

Where_____

When_____

DATE NIGHT

What_____

Where_____

When_____

DATE NIGHT

What_____

Where_____

When_____

DATE NIGHT

What_____

Where_____

When_____

DATE NIGHT

What_____

Where_____

When_____

DATE NIGHT

What_____

Where_____

When_____

DATE NIGHT

What_____

Where_____

When_____

• • • • • • • ● ● ● ● ♡ ● ● ● ● • • • • •

THINGS TO DO

Pickup

Calls

Sitter

THINGS TO DO

Pickup

Calls

Sitter

THINGS TO DO

Pickup

Calls

Sitter

MONTH _____

• • • • • • • ● ● ● ● ♡ ● ● ● • • • • •

DATE NIGHT

What _____

Where _____

When _____

DATE NIGHT

What _____

Where _____

When _____

DATE NIGHT

What _____

Where _____

When _____

DATE NIGHT

What _____

Where _____

When _____

DATE NIGHT

What _____

Where _____

When _____

DATE NIGHT

What _____

Where _____

When _____

DATE NIGHT

What _____

Where _____

When _____

DATE NIGHT

What _____

Where _____

When _____

DATE NIGHT

What _____

Where _____

When _____

• • • • • • • ● ● ● ♡ ● ● ● • • • • •

THINGS TO DO

Pickup

Calls

Sitter

THINGS TO DO

Pickup

Calls

Sitter

THINGS TO DO

Pickup

Calls

Sitter

MONTH _____

•••••●●●●●♡●●●●●●•••

DATE NIGHT

What _____

Where _____

When _____

DATE NIGHT

What _____

Where _____

When _____

DATE NIGHT

What _____

Where _____

When _____

DATE NIGHT

What _____

Where _____

When _____

DATE NIGHT

What _____

Where _____

When _____

DATE NIGHT

What _____

Where _____

When _____

DATE NIGHT

What _____

Where _____

When _____

DATE NIGHT

What _____

Where _____

When _____

DATE NIGHT

What _____

Where _____

When _____

•••••●●●●●♡●●●●●●•••

THINGS TO DO

Pickup

Calls

Sitter

THINGS TO DO

Pickup

Calls

Sitter

THINGS TO DO

Pickup

Calls

Sitter

MONTH _____

• • • • • ● ● ● ● ● ♡ ● ● ● ● • • • •

DATE NIGHT

What_____

Where_____

When_____

DATE NIGHT

What_____

Where_____

When_____

DATE NIGHT

What_____

Where_____

When_____

DATE NIGHT

What_____

Where_____

When_____

DATE NIGHT

What_____

Where_____

When_____

DATE NIGHT

What_____

Where_____

When_____

DATE NIGHT

What_____

Where_____

When_____

DATE NIGHT

What_____

Where_____

When_____

DATE NIGHT

What_____

Where_____

When_____

• • • • • ● ● ● ● ● ♡ ● ● ● ● • • • •

THINGS TO DO

Pickup

Calls

Sitter

THINGS TO DO

Pickup

Calls

Sitter

THINGS TO DO

Pickup

Calls

Sitter

MONTH _____

• • • • • • • • • ● ♡ ● • • • • • • •

DATE NIGHT	DATE NIGHT	DATE NIGHT
What _____	*What* _____	*What* _____
Where _____	*Where* _____	*Where* _____
When _____	*When* _____	*When* _____

DATE NIGHT	DATE NIGHT	DATE NIGHT
What _____	*What* _____	*What* _____
Where _____	*Where* _____	*Where* _____
When _____	*When* _____	*When* _____

DATE NIGHT	DATE NIGHT	DATE NIGHT
What _____	*What* _____	*What* _____
Where _____	*Where* _____	*Where* _____
When _____	*When* _____	*When* _____

• • • • • • • • • ● ♡ ● • • • • • • •

THINGS TO DO	THINGS TO DO	THINGS TO DO
Pickup	*Pickup*	*Pickup*
Calls	*Calls*	*Calls*
Sitter	*Sitter*	*Sitter*

MONTH _____

• • • • • ● ● ● ● ● ♡ ● ● ● ● • • • •

DATE NIGHT	DATE NIGHT	DATE NIGHT
What _____	What _____	What _____
Where _____	Where _____	Where _____
When _____	When _____	When _____
DATE NIGHT	DATE NIGHT	DATE NIGHT
What _____	What _____	What _____
Where _____	Where _____	Where _____
When _____	When _____	When _____
DATE NIGHT	DATE NIGHT	DATE NIGHT
What _____	What _____	What _____
Where _____	Where _____	Where _____
When _____	When _____	When _____

• • • • • ● ● ● ● ● ♡ ● ● ● ● • • • •

THINGS TO DO	THINGS TO DO	THINGS TO DO
Pickup	Pickup	Pickup
Calls	Calls	Calls
Sitter	Sitter	Sitter

MONTH _____

• • • • • • • ● ● ● ● ♡ ● ● ● • • • • •

DATE NIGHT	DATE NIGHT	DATE NIGHT
What _____	What _____	What _____
Where _____	Where _____	Where _____
When _____	When _____	When _____

DATE NIGHT	DATE NIGHT	DATE NIGHT
What _____	What _____	What _____
Where _____	Where _____	Where _____
When _____	When _____	When _____

DATE NIGHT	DATE NIGHT	DATE NIGHT
What _____	What _____	What _____
Where _____	Where _____	Where _____
When _____	When _____	When _____

• • • • • • • ● ● ● ● ♡ ● ● ● • • • • •

THINGS TO DO	THINGS TO DO	THINGS TO DO
Pickup	Pickup	Pickup
Calls	Calls	Calls
Sitter	Sitter	Sitter

MONTH _____

• • • • • • • ● ● ● ● ● ♡ ● ● ● ● ● • • • •

DATE NIGHT	DATE NIGHT	DATE NIGHT
What _____	*What* _____	*What* _____
Where _____	*Where* _____	*Where* _____
When _____	*When* _____	*When* _____

DATE NIGHT	DATE NIGHT	DATE NIGHT
What _____	*What* _____	*What* _____
Where _____	*Where* _____	*Where* _____
When _____	*When* _____	*When* _____

DATE NIGHT	DATE NIGHT	DATE NIGHT
What _____	*What* _____	*What* _____
Where _____	*Where* _____	*Where* _____
When _____	*When* _____	*When* _____

• • • • • • • ● ● ● ● ● ♡ ● ● ● ● ● • • • •

THINGS TO DO	THINGS TO DO	THINGS TO DO
Pickup	*Pickup*	*Pickup*
Calls	*Calls*	*Calls*
Sitter	*Sitter*	*Sitter*

MONTH _____

•••••●●●●●♡●●●●●•••

DATE NIGHT	DATE NIGHT	DATE NIGHT
What_____	What_____	What_____
Where_____	Where_____	Where_____
When_____	When_____	When_____

DATE NIGHT	DATE NIGHT	DATE NIGHT
What_____	What_____	What_____
Where_____	Where_____	Where_____
When_____	When_____	When_____

DATE NIGHT	DATE NIGHT	DATE NIGHT
What_____	What_____	What_____
Where_____	Where_____	Where_____
When_____	When_____	When_____

•••••●●●●●♡●●●●●•••

THINGS TO DO	THINGS TO DO	THINGS TO DO
Pickup	Pickup	Pickup
Calls	Calls	Calls
Sitter	Sitter	Sitter

MONTH _____

• • • • • • • ● ● ● ● ♡ ● ● ● ● • • • •

DATE NIGHT	DATE NIGHT	DATE NIGHT
What _____	What _____	What _____
Where _____	Where _____	Where _____
When _____	When _____	When _____

DATE NIGHT	DATE NIGHT	DATE NIGHT
What _____	What _____	What _____
Where _____	Where _____	Where _____
When _____	When _____	When _____

DATE NIGHT	DATE NIGHT	DATE NIGHT
What _____	What _____	What _____
Where _____	Where _____	Where _____
When _____	When _____	When _____

• • • • • • • ● ● ● ● ♡ ● ● ● ● • • • •

THINGS TO DO	THINGS TO DO	THINGS TO DO
Pickup	Pickup	Pickup
Calls	Calls	Calls
Sitter	Sitter	Sitter

MONTH _____

•••••••●●●●●♡●●●●••••••

DATE NIGHT

What _____

Where _____

When _____

DATE NIGHT

What _____

Where _____

When _____

DATE NIGHT

What _____

Where _____

When _____

DATE NIGHT

What _____

Where _____

When _____

DATE NIGHT

What _____

Where _____

When _____

DATE NIGHT

What _____

Where _____

When _____

DATE NIGHT

What _____

Where _____

When _____

DATE NIGHT

What _____

Where _____

When _____

DATE NIGHT

What _____

Where _____

When _____

•••••••●●●●●♡●●●●••••••

THINGS TO DO

Pickup

Calls

Sitter

THINGS TO DO

Pickup

Calls

Sitter

THINGS TO DO

Pickup

Calls

Sitter

MONTH _____

•••••••●●●●●●◉♡◉●●●●●●•••••

DATE NIGHT

What _____

Where _____

When _____

DATE NIGHT

What _____

Where _____

When _____

DATE NIGHT

What _____

Where _____

When _____

DATE NIGHT

What _____

Where _____

When _____

DATE NIGHT

What _____

Where _____

When _____

DATE NIGHT

What _____

Where _____

When _____

DATE NIGHT

What _____

Where _____

When _____

DATE NIGHT

What _____

Where _____

When _____

DATE NIGHT

What _____

Where _____

When _____

•••••••●●●●●●◉♡◉●●●●●●•••••

THINGS TO DO

Pickup

Calls

Sitter

THINGS TO DO

Pickup

Calls

Sitter

THINGS TO DO

Pickup

Calls

Sitter

MONTH _____

·········●●●●●●♡●●●●●·········

DATE NIGHT

What_____

Where_____

When_____

DATE NIGHT

What_____

Where_____

When_____

DATE NIGHT

What_____

Where_____

When_____

DATE NIGHT

What_____

Where_____

When_____

DATE NIGHT

What_____

Where_____

When_____

DATE NIGHT

What_____

Where_____

When_____

DATE NIGHT

What_____

Where_____

When_____

DATE NIGHT

What_____

Where_____

When_____

DATE NIGHT

What_____

Where_____

When_____

·········●●●●●●♡●●●●●·········

THINGS TO DO

Pickup

Calls

Sitter

THINGS TO DO

Pickup

Calls

Sitter

THINGS TO DO

Pickup

Calls

Sitter

MONTH _____

•••••●●●●●●♡●●●●●•••••

DATE NIGHT

What _____

Where _____

When _____

DATE NIGHT

What _____

Where _____

When _____

DATE NIGHT

What _____

Where _____

When _____

DATE NIGHT

What _____

Where _____

When _____

DATE NIGHT

What _____

Where _____

When _____

DATE NIGHT

What _____

Where _____

When _____

DATE NIGHT

What _____

Where _____

When _____

DATE NIGHT

What _____

Where _____

When _____

DATE NIGHT

What _____

Where _____

When _____

•••••●●●●●♡●●●●●•••••

THINGS TO DO

Pickup

Calls

Sitter

THINGS TO DO

Pickup

Calls

Sitter

THINGS TO DO

Pickup

Calls

Sitter

MONTH _____

•••••●●●●●●♡●●●●●●••••

DATE NIGHT	DATE NIGHT	DATE NIGHT
What _____	*What* _____	*What* _____
Where _____	*Where* _____	*Where* _____
When _____	*When* _____	*When* _____

DATE NIGHT	DATE NIGHT	DATE NIGHT
What _____	*What* _____	*What* _____
Where _____	*Where* _____	*Where* _____
When _____	*When* _____	*When* _____

DATE NIGHT	DATE NIGHT	DATE NIGHT
What _____	*What* _____	*What* _____
Where _____	*Where* _____	*Where* _____
When _____	*When* _____	*When* _____

•••••●●●●●●♡●●●●●●••••

THINGS TO DO	THINGS TO DO	THINGS TO DO
Pickup	*Pickup*	*Pickup*
Calls	*Calls*	*Calls*
Sitter	*Sitter*	*Sitter*

MONTH _____

• • • • • • ● ● ● ● ♡ ● ● ● ● • • • •

DATE NIGHT

What_____
Where_____
When_____

DATE NIGHT

What_____
Where_____
When_____

DATE NIGHT

What_____
Where_____
When_____

DATE NIGHT

What_____
Where_____
When_____

DATE NIGHT

What_____
Where_____
When_____

DATE NIGHT

What_____
Where_____
When_____

DATE NIGHT

What_____
Where_____
When_____

DATE NIGHT

What_____
Where_____
When_____

DATE NIGHT

What_____
Where_____
When_____

• • • • • • ● ● ● ● ♡ ● ● ● ● • • • •

THINGS TO DO

Pickup

Calls

Sitter

THINGS TO DO

Pickup

Calls

Sitter

THINGS TO DO

Pickup

Calls

Sitter

MONTH _____

•••••●●●●●●♡●●●●●•••••

DATE NIGHT

What _____

Where _____

When _____

DATE NIGHT

What _____

Where _____

When _____

DATE NIGHT

What _____

Where _____

When _____

DATE NIGHT

What _____

Where _____

When _____

DATE NIGHT

What _____

Where _____

When _____

DATE NIGHT

What _____

Where _____

When _____

DATE NIGHT

What _____

Where _____

When _____

DATE NIGHT

What _____

Where _____

When _____

DATE NIGHT

What _____

Where _____

When _____

•••••●●●●●●♡●●●●●•••••

THINGS TO DO

Pickup

Calls

Sitter

THINGS TO DO

Pickup

Calls

Sitter

THINGS TO DO

Pickup

Calls

Sitter

MONTH _____

•••••••●●●●●●♡●●●●●●•••••

DATE NIGHT

What _____

Where _____

When _____

DATE NIGHT

What _____

Where _____

When _____

DATE NIGHT

What _____

Where _____

When _____

DATE NIGHT

What _____

Where _____

When _____

DATE NIGHT

What _____

Where _____

When _____

DATE NIGHT

What _____

Where _____

When _____

DATE NIGHT

What _____

Where _____

When _____

DATE NIGHT

What _____

Where _____

When _____

DATE NIGHT

What _____

Where _____

When _____

•••••••●●●●●♡●●●●●●•••••

THINGS TO DO

Pickup

Calls

Sitter

THINGS TO DO

Pickup

Calls

Sitter

THINGS TO DO

Pickup

Calls

Sitter

MONTH _____

•••••●●●●●●♡●●●●●●••••

| DATE NIGHT | DATE NIGHT | DATE NIGHT |

What _____

Where _____

When _____

What _____

Where _____

When _____

What _____

Where _____

When _____

DATE NIGHT   DATE NIGHT   DATE NIGHT

What _____

Where _____

When _____

What _____

Where _____

When _____

What _____

Where _____

When _____

DATE NIGHT   DATE NIGHT   DATE NIGHT

What _____

Where _____

When _____

What _____

Where _____

When _____

What _____

Where _____

When _____

•••••●●●●●●♡●●●●●●••••

THINGS TO DO   THINGS TO DO   THINGS TO DO

Pickup   *Pickup*   *Pickup*

Calls   *Calls*   *Calls*

Sitter   *Sitter*   *Sitter*

MONTH _____

· · · · · • • • ● ● ♡ ● ● • • • · · · ·

DATE NIGHT

What _____

Where _____

When _____

DATE NIGHT

What _____

Where _____

When _____

DATE NIGHT

What _____

Where _____

When _____

DATE NIGHT

What _____

Where _____

When _____

DATE NIGHT

What _____

Where _____

When _____

DATE NIGHT

What _____

Where _____

When _____

DATE NIGHT

What _____

Where _____

When _____

DATE NIGHT

What _____

Where _____

When _____

DATE NIGHT

What _____

Where _____

When _____

· · · · · • • • ● ● ♡ ● ● • • • · · · ·

THINGS TO DO

Pickup

Calls

Sitter

THINGS TO DO

Pickup

Calls

Sitter

THINGS TO DO

Pickup

Calls

Sitter

MONTH _____

•••••••●●●●●●♡●●●●●●•••••

DATE NIGHT

What_____

Where_____

When_____

DATE NIGHT

What_____

Where_____

When_____

DATE NIGHT

What_____

Where_____

When_____

DATE NIGHT

What_____

Where_____

When_____

DATE NIGHT

What_____

Where_____

When_____

DATE NIGHT

What_____

Where_____

When_____

DATE NIGHT

What_____

Where_____

When_____

DATE NIGHT

What_____

Where_____

When_____

DATE NIGHT

What_____

Where_____

When_____

•••••••●●●●●●♡●●●●●●•••••

THINGS TO DO

Pickup

Calls

Sitter

THINGS TO DO

Pickup

Calls

Sitter

THINGS TO DO

Pickup

Calls

Sitter

MONTH _____

•••••●●●●●●♡●●●●●●•••••

DATE NIGHT

What_____

Where_____

When_____

DATE NIGHT

What_____

Where_____

When_____

DATE NIGHT

What_____

Where_____

When_____

DATE NIGHT

What_____

Where_____

When_____

DATE NIGHT

What_____

Where_____

When_____

DATE NIGHT

What_____

Where_____

When_____

DATE NIGHT

What_____

Where_____

When_____

DATE NIGHT

What_____

Where_____

When_____

DATE NIGHT

What_____

Where_____

When_____

•••••●●●●●●♡●●●●●●•••••

THINGS TO DO

Pickup

Calls

Sitter

THINGS TO DO

Pickup

Calls

Sitter

THINGS TO DO

Pickup

Calls

Sitter

MONTH _____

•••••••●●●●●●♡●●●●●●•••••

DATE NIGHT	DATE NIGHT	DATE NIGHT
What _____	What _____	What _____
Where _____	Where _____	Where _____
When _____	When _____	When _____

DATE NIGHT	DATE NIGHT	DATE NIGHT
What _____	What _____	What _____
Where _____	Where _____	Where _____
When _____	When _____	When _____

DATE NIGHT	DATE NIGHT	DATE NIGHT
What _____	What _____	What _____
Where _____	Where _____	Where _____
When _____	When _____	When _____

•••••••●●●●●●♡●●●●●●•••••

THINGS TO DO	THINGS TO DO	THINGS TO DO
Pickup	Pickup	Pickup
Calls	Calls	Calls
Sitter	Sitter	Sitter

MONTH _____

•••••●●●●♡●●●●•••••

DATE NIGHT	DATE NIGHT	DATE NIGHT
What _____	*What* _____	*What* _____
Where _____	*Where* _____	*Where* _____
When _____	*When* _____	*When* _____

DATE NIGHT	DATE NIGHT	DATE NIGHT
What _____	*What* _____	*What* _____
Where _____	*Where* _____	*Where* _____
When _____	*When* _____	*When* _____

DATE NIGHT	DATE NIGHT	DATE NIGHT
What _____	*What* _____	*What* _____
Where _____	*Where* _____	*Where* _____
When _____	*When* _____	*When* _____

•••••●●●●♡●●●●•••••

THINGS TO DO	THINGS TO DO	THINGS TO DO
Pickup	*Pickup*	*Pickup*
Calls	*Calls*	*Calls*
Sitter	*Sitter*	*Sitter*

MONTH _____

•••••●●●●●●●♡●●●●●●•••••

DATE NIGHT

What _____

Where _____

When _____

DATE NIGHT

What _____

Where _____

When _____

DATE NIGHT

What _____

Where _____

When _____

DATE NIGHT

What _____

Where _____

When _____

DATE NIGHT

What _____

Where _____

When _____

DATE NIGHT

What _____

Where _____

When _____

DATE NIGHT

What _____

Where _____

When _____

DATE NIGHT

What _____

Where _____

When _____

DATE NIGHT

What _____

Where _____

When _____

•••••●●●●●●●♡●●●●●●•••••

THINGS TO DO

Pickup

Calls

Sitter

THINGS TO DO

Pickup

Calls

Sitter

THINGS TO DO

Pickup

Calls

Sitter

MONTH _____

· · · · · · • • ● ● ● ♡ ● ● ● • • · · · ·

DATE NIGHT

What_____

Where_____

When_____

DATE NIGHT

What_____

Where_____

When_____

DATE NIGHT

What_____

Where_____

When_____

DATE NIGHT

What_____

Where_____

When_____

DATE NIGHT

What_____

Where_____

When_____

DATE NIGHT

What_____

Where_____

When_____

DATE NIGHT

What_____

Where_____

When_____

DATE NIGHT

What_____

Where_____

When_____

DATE NIGHT

What_____

Where_____

When_____

· · · · · · • • ● ● ● ♡ ● ● ● • • · · · ·

THINGS TO DO

Pickup

Calls

Sitter

THINGS TO DO

Pickup

Calls

Sitter

THINGS TO DO

Pickup

Calls

Sitter

MONTH _____

•••••••●●●●♡●●●●•••••

DATE NIGHT	DATE NIGHT	DATE NIGHT
What _____	What _____	What _____
Where _____	Where _____	Where _____
When _____	When _____	When _____

DATE NIGHT	DATE NIGHT	DATE NIGHT
What _____	What _____	What _____
Where _____	Where _____	Where _____
When _____	When _____	When _____

DATE NIGHT	DATE NIGHT	DATE NIGHT
What _____	What _____	What _____
Where _____	Where _____	Where _____
When _____	When _____	When _____

•••••••●●●●♡●●●●•••••

THINGS TO DO	THINGS TO DO	THINGS TO DO
Pickup	Pickup	Pickup
Calls	Calls	Calls
Sitter	Sitter	Sitter

MONTH _____

•••••●●●●●♡●●●●●•••

DATE NIGHT

What _____

Where _____

When _____

DATE NIGHT

What _____

Where _____

When _____

DATE NIGHT

What _____

Where _____

When _____

DATE NIGHT

What _____

Where _____

When _____

DATE NIGHT

What _____

Where _____

When _____

DATE NIGHT

What _____

Where _____

When _____

DATE NIGHT

What _____

Where _____

When _____

DATE NIGHT

What _____

Where _____

When _____

DATE NIGHT

What _____

Where _____

When _____

•••••●●●●●♡●●●●●•••

THINGS TO DO

Pickup

Calls

Sitter

THINGS TO DO

Pickup

Calls

Sitter

THINGS TO DO

Pickup

Calls

Sitter

MONTH _____

• • • • • • • ● ● ● ● ● ♡ ● ● ● ● ● • • • •

DATE NIGHT

What_____
Where_____
When_____

DATE NIGHT

What_____
Where_____
When_____

DATE NIGHT

What_____
Where_____
When_____

DATE NIGHT

What_____
Where_____
When_____

DATE NIGHT

What_____
Where_____
When_____

DATE NIGHT

What_____
Where_____
When_____

DATE NIGHT

What_____
Where_____
When_____

DATE NIGHT

What_____
Where_____
When_____

DATE NIGHT

What_____
Where_____
When_____

• • • • • • • ● ● ● ● ● ♡ ● ● ● ● ● • • • •

THINGS TO DO

Pickup

Calls

Sitter

THINGS TO DO

Pickup

Calls

Sitter

THINGS TO DO

Pickup

Calls

Sitter

MONTH _____

• • • • • • • • • ● ● ● ♡ ● ● ● ● • • • • •

DATE NIGHT	DATE NIGHT	DATE NIGHT
What _____	What _____	What _____
Where _____	Where _____	Where _____
When _____	When _____	When _____

DATE NIGHT	DATE NIGHT	DATE NIGHT
What _____	What _____	What _____
Where _____	Where _____	Where _____
When _____	When _____	When _____

DATE NIGHT	DATE NIGHT	DATE NIGHT
What _____	What _____	What _____
Where _____	Where _____	Where _____
When _____	When _____	When _____

• • • • • • • • ● ● ● ♡ ● ● ● ● • • • •

THINGS TO DO	THINGS TO DO	THINGS TO DO
Pickup	Pickup	Pickup
Calls	Calls	Calls
Sitter	Sitter	Sitter

MONTH _____

•••••••●●●●●●♡●●●●●•••••

DATE NIGHT

What_____

Where_____

When_____

DATE NIGHT

What_____

Where_____

When_____

DATE NIGHT

What_____

Where_____

When_____

DATE NIGHT

What_____

Where_____

When_____

DATE NIGHT

What_____

Where_____

When_____

DATE NIGHT

What_____

Where_____

When_____

DATE NIGHT

What_____

Where_____

When_____

DATE NIGHT

What_____

Where_____

When_____

DATE NIGHT

What_____

Where_____

When_____

•••••••●●●●●●♡●●●●●•••••

THINGS TO DO

Pickup

Calls

Sitter

THINGS TO DO

Pickup

Calls

Sitter

THINGS TO DO

Pickup

Calls

Sitter

MONTH _____

•••••••●●●●●♡●●●●••••••

DATE NIGHT	DATE NIGHT	DATE NIGHT
What _____	*What* _____	*What* _____
Where _____	*Where* _____	*Where* _____
When _____	*When* _____	*When* _____

DATE NIGHT	DATE NIGHT	DATE NIGHT
What _____	*What* _____	*What* _____
Where _____	*Where* _____	*Where* _____
When _____	*When* _____	*When* _____

DATE NIGHT	DATE NIGHT	DATE NIGHT
What _____	*What* _____	*What* _____
Where _____	*Where* _____	*Where* _____
When _____	*When* _____	*When* _____

•••••••●●●●♡●●●●•••••••

THINGS TO DO	THINGS TO DO	THINGS TO DO
Pickup	*Pickup*	*Pickup*
Calls	*Calls*	*Calls*
Sitter	*Sitter*	*Sitter*

MONTH _____

•••••●●●●●●❤●●●●●●•••

DATE NIGHT

What _____
Where _____
When _____

DATE NIGHT

What _____
Where _____
When _____

DATE NIGHT

What _____
Where _____
When _____

DATE NIGHT

What _____
Where _____
When _____

DATE NIGHT

What _____
Where _____
When _____

DATE NIGHT

What _____
Where _____
When _____

DATE NIGHT

What _____
Where _____
When _____

DATE NIGHT

What _____
Where _____
When _____

DATE NIGHT

What _____
Where _____
When _____

•••••●●●●●●❤●●●●●●•••

THINGS TO DO

Pickup

Calls

Sitter

THINGS TO DO

Pickup

Calls

Sitter

THINGS TO DO

Pickup

Calls

Sitter

MONTH _____

• • • • • • • ● ● ● ● ♡ ● ● ● ● • • • •

DATE NIGHT

What _____

Where _____

When _____

DATE NIGHT

What _____

Where _____

When _____

DATE NIGHT

What _____

Where _____

When _____

DATE NIGHT

What _____

Where _____

When _____

DATE NIGHT

What _____

Where _____

When _____

DATE NIGHT

What _____

Where _____

When _____

DATE NIGHT

What _____

Where _____

When _____

DATE NIGHT

What _____

Where _____

When _____

DATE NIGHT

What _____

Where _____

When _____

• • • • • • • ● ● ● ● ♡ ● ● ● ● • • • •

THINGS TO DO

Pickup

Calls

Sitter

THINGS TO DO

Pickup

Calls

Sitter

THINGS TO DO

Pickup

Calls

Sitter

MONTH _____

• • • • • • • • • • ♡ • • • • • • • • •

DATE NIGHT

What_____

Where_____

When_____

DATE NIGHT

What_____

Where_____

When_____

DATE NIGHT

What_____

Where_____

When_____

DATE NIGHT

What_____

Where_____

When_____

DATE NIGHT

What_____

Where_____

When_____

DATE NIGHT

What_____

Where_____

When_____

DATE NIGHT

What_____

Where_____

When_____

DATE NIGHT

What_____

Where_____

When_____

DATE NIGHT

What_____

Where_____

When_____

• • • • • • • • • • ♡ • • • • • • • • •

THINGS TO DO

Pickup

Calls

Sitter

THINGS TO DO

Pickup

Calls

Sitter

THINGS TO DO

Pickup

Calls

Sitter

MONTH _____

•••••••●●●●♡●●●●●•••••

DATE NIGHT	DATE NIGHT	DATE NIGHT
What _____	*What* _____	*What* _____
Where _____	*Where* _____	*Where* _____
When _____	*When* _____	*When* _____

DATE NIGHT	DATE NIGHT	DATE NIGHT
What _____	*What* _____	*What* _____
Where _____	*Where* _____	*Where* _____
When _____	*When* _____	*When* _____

DATE NIGHT	DATE NIGHT	DATE NIGHT
What _____	*What* _____	*What* _____
Where _____	*Where* _____	*Where* _____
When _____	*When* _____	*When* _____

•••••••●●●♡●●●●•••••

THINGS TO DO	THINGS TO DO	THINGS TO DO
Pickup	*Pickup*	*Pickup*
Calls	*Calls*	*Calls*
Sitter	*Sitter*	*Sitter*

MONTH _____

• • • • • • • • • ● ● ● ● ♡ ● ● ● • • • • • • •

DATE NIGHT

What _____

Where _____

When _____

DATE NIGHT

What _____

Where _____

When _____

DATE NIGHT

What _____

Where _____

When _____

DATE NIGHT

What _____

Where _____

When _____

DATE NIGHT

What _____

Where _____

When _____

DATE NIGHT

What _____

Where _____

When _____

DATE NIGHT

What _____

Where _____

When _____

DATE NIGHT

What _____

Where _____

When _____

DATE NIGHT

What _____

Where _____

When _____

• • • • • • • • ● ● ● ● ♡ ● ● ● • • • • • • •

THINGS TO DO

Pickup

Calls

Sitter

THINGS TO DO

Pickup

Calls

Sitter

THINGS TO DO

Pickup

Calls

Sitter

MONTH _____

•••••●●●●●●●♡●●●●●●•••••

DATE NIGHT

What _____

Where _____

When _____

DATE NIGHT

What _____

Where _____

When _____

DATE NIGHT

What _____

Where _____

When _____

DATE NIGHT

What _____

Where _____

When _____

DATE NIGHT

What _____

Where _____

When _____

DATE NIGHT

What _____

Where _____

When _____

DATE NIGHT

What _____

Where _____

When _____

DATE NIGHT

What _____

Where _____

When _____

DATE NIGHT

What _____

Where _____

When _____

•••••●●●●●●●♡●●●●●●•••••

THINGS TO DO

Pickup

Calls

Sitter

THINGS TO DO

Pickup

Calls

Sitter

THINGS TO DO

Pickup

Calls

Sitter

MONTH _____

•••••••●●●●●●●♡●●●●●●•••••

DATE NIGHT

What _____

Where _____

When _____

DATE NIGHT

What _____

Where _____

When _____

DATE NIGHT

What _____

Where _____

When _____

DATE NIGHT

What _____

Where _____

When _____

DATE NIGHT

What _____

Where _____

When _____

DATE NIGHT

What _____

Where _____

When _____

DATE NIGHT

What _____

Where _____

When _____

DATE NIGHT

What _____

Where _____

When _____

DATE NIGHT

What _____

Where _____

When _____

•••••••●●●●●●●♡●●●●●●•••••

THINGS TO DO

Pickup

Calls

Sitter

THINGS TO DO

Pickup

Calls

Sitter

THINGS TO DO

Pickup

Calls

Sitter

MONTH _____

•••• • • • ● ● ● ♡ ● ● • • • ••••

DATE NIGHT

*What*_____

*Where*_____

*When*_____

DATE NIGHT

*What*_____

*Where*_____

*When*_____

DATE NIGHT

*What*_____

*Where*_____

*When*_____

DATE NIGHT

*What*_____

*Where*_____

*When*_____

DATE NIGHT

*What*_____

*Where*_____

*When*_____

DATE NIGHT

*What*_____

*Where*_____

*When*_____

DATE NIGHT

*What*_____

*Where*_____

*When*_____

DATE NIGHT

*What*_____

*Where*_____

*When*_____

DATE NIGHT

*What*_____

*Where*_____

*When*_____

•••• • • • ● ● ● ♡ ● ● • • • ••••

THINGS TO DO

Pickup

Calls

Sitter

THINGS TO DO

Pickup

Calls

Sitter

THINGS TO DO

Pickup

Calls

Sitter

MONTH _____

• • • • • • • • ● ● ● ● ● ● ♡ ● ● ● ● ● • • • •

DATE NIGHT

What _____
Where _____
When _____

DATE NIGHT

What _____
Where _____
When _____

DATE NIGHT

What _____
Where _____
When _____

DATE NIGHT

What _____
Where _____
When _____

DATE NIGHT

What _____
Where _____
When _____

DATE NIGHT

What _____
Where _____
When _____

DATE NIGHT

What _____
Where _____
When _____

DATE NIGHT

What _____
Where _____
When _____

DATE NIGHT

What _____
Where _____
When _____

• • • • • • • • ● ● ● ● ● ● ♡ ● ● ● ● ● • • • •

THINGS TO DO

Pickup

Calls

Sitter

THINGS TO DO

Pickup

Calls

Sitter

THINGS TO DO

Pickup

Calls

Sitter

MONTH _____

•••••••●●●●●♡●●●●●•••••

DATE NIGHT	DATE NIGHT	DATE NIGHT
What _____	What _____	What _____
Where _____	Where _____	Where _____
When _____	When _____	When _____

DATE NIGHT	DATE NIGHT	DATE NIGHT
What _____	What _____	What _____
Where _____	Where _____	Where _____
When _____	When _____	When _____

DATE NIGHT	DATE NIGHT	DATE NIGHT
What _____	What _____	What _____
Where _____	Where _____	Where _____
When _____	When _____	When _____

•••••••●●●●●♡●●●●●•••••

THINGS TO DO	THINGS TO DO	THINGS TO DO
Pickup	Pickup	Pickup
Calls	Calls	Calls
Sitter	Sitter	Sitter

MONTH _____

• • • • • • • • ● ● ♡ ● ● ● • • • • • •

DATE NIGHT

What_____

Where_____

When_____

DATE NIGHT

What_____

Where_____

When_____

DATE NIGHT

What_____

Where_____

When_____

DATE NIGHT

What_____

Where_____

When_____

DATE NIGHT

What_____

Where_____

When_____

DATE NIGHT

What_____

Where_____

When_____

DATE NIGHT

What_____

Where_____

When_____

DATE NIGHT

What_____

Where_____

When_____

DATE NIGHT

What_____

Where_____

When_____

• • • • • • • ● ● ● ♡ ● ● ● • • • • •

THINGS TO DO

Pickup

Calls

Sitter

THINGS TO DO

Pickup

Calls

Sitter

THINGS TO DO

Pickup

Calls

Sitter

MONTH _____

•••••••••●●●♡●●●●●●•••••

DATE NIGHT

What _____

Where _____

When _____

DATE NIGHT

What _____

Where _____

When _____

DATE NIGHT

What _____

Where _____

When _____

DATE NIGHT

What _____

Where _____

When _____

DATE NIGHT

What _____

Where _____

When _____

DATE NIGHT

What _____

Where _____

When _____

DATE NIGHT

What _____

Where _____

When _____

DATE NIGHT

What _____

Where _____

When _____

DATE NIGHT

What _____

Where _____

When _____

•••••••••●●●♡●●●●●●•••••

THINGS TO DO

Pickup

Calls

Sitter

THINGS TO DO

Pickup

Calls

Sitter

THINGS TO DO

Pickup

Calls

Sitter

MONTH _____

•••••••●●●●♡●●●●●•••••

DATE NIGHT	DATE NIGHT	DATE NIGHT

DATE NIGHT

What _____

Where _____

When _____

DATE NIGHT

What _____

Where _____

When _____

DATE NIGHT

What _____

Where _____

When _____

DATE NIGHT

What _____

Where _____

When _____

DATE NIGHT

What _____

Where _____

When _____

DATE NIGHT

What _____

Where _____

When _____

DATE NIGHT

What _____

Where _____

When _____

DATE NIGHT

What _____

Where _____

When _____

DATE NIGHT

What _____

Where _____

When _____

•••••••●●●●♡●●●●●•••••

THINGS TO DO

Pickup

Calls

Sitter

THINGS TO DO

Pickup

Calls

Sitter

THINGS TO DO

Pickup

Calls

Sitter

MONTH _____

• • • • • • • • ● ● ● ♡ ● ● ● • • • •

DATE NIGHT

What _____

Where _____

When _____

DATE NIGHT

What _____

Where _____

When _____

DATE NIGHT

What _____

Where _____

When _____

DATE NIGHT

What _____

Where _____

When _____

DATE NIGHT

What _____

Where _____

When _____

DATE NIGHT

What _____

Where _____

When _____

DATE NIGHT

What _____

Where _____

When _____

DATE NIGHT

What _____

Where _____

When _____

DATE NIGHT

What _____

Where _____

When _____

• • • • • • • ● ● ● ♡ ● ● ● • • • • •

THINGS TO DO

Pickup

Calls

Sitter

THINGS TO DO

Pickup

Calls

Sitter

THINGS TO DO

Pickup

Calls

Sitter